peak mathematics **1**

Alan Brighouse
David Godber
Peter Patilla

Nelson

Thomas Nelson and Sons Ltd
Nelson House Mayfield Road
Walton-on-Thames Surrey
KT12 5PL UK

51 York Place
Edinburgh EH1 3JD UK

Thomas Nelson (Hong Kong) Ltd
Toppan Building 10/F 22A Westlands Road
Quarry Bay Hong Kong

Distributed in Australia by

Thomas Nelson Australia
480 La Trobe Street
Melbourne Victoria 3000
and in Sydney, Brisbane, Adelaide and Perth

Nelson Canada
1120 Birchmount Road
Scarborough Ontario
M1K 5G4 Canada

First published 1981 by Thomas Nelson and Sons Ltd

ISBN 0-17-421306-9

NPN 19 18 17 16 15 14 13 12 11 10

Printed in Hong Kong

Filmset in the Nelson Teaching Alphabet
by Mould Type Foundry Ltd
Brookfield Street Preston England

Art Direction   Sharon Lovett, Michael Kaufmann

Design   Sharon Lovett, Sylvia Tate, Julia Denny

Photography   Chris Ridgers, Dawson Strange, Janine Wiedel

Cover Photography   Colorific

Illustration   Christine Roche, Simon Stern

Photographic props courtesy of Hestair Hope Ltd.,
Britains' Toys Ltd., and ESA Ltd.

Contents

Addition

Write these numbers in words.

1. 15
2. 19
3. 34
4. 60
5. 40
6. 75
7. 109
8. 101
9. 259

Write these numbers in figures.

1. twenty
2. fifty
3. eighty
4. one hundred
5. thirteen
6. sixteen
7. nineteen
8. thirty-nine
9. two hundred and four
10. three hundred and twenty
11. one hundred and fifty-eight
12. four hundred and fifty-six
13. five hundred and sixty-two
14. eight hundred and nine
15. seven hundred and forty-seven
16. nine hundred and twenty-eight

Write the value of the number in red.

17. 3 4 7 → 4 tens → 40
18. 53 4
19. 2 03
20. 9 7
21. 4 1 9
22. 6 94
23. 4 09
24. 76 0
25. 5 1 1
26. 7 8
27. 6 25
28. 89 9
29. 6 1 5
30. 8 9

Addition

Write the numbers these abaci show.

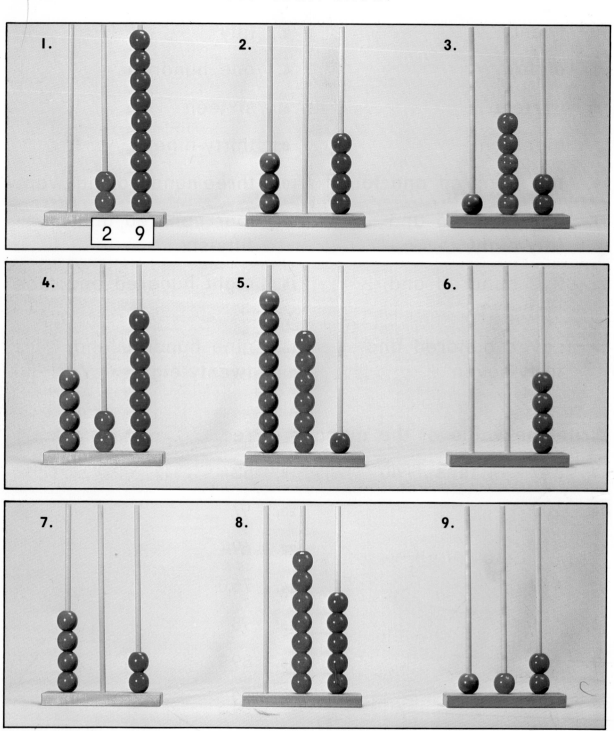

1. | 2 | 9 |

6

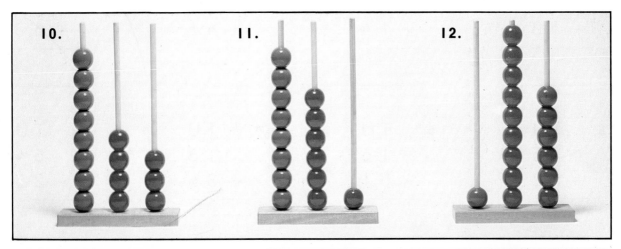

Draw 12 abaci.

Draw these numbers on your abaci.

16.

1 7

17. 346

18. 89

19. 708

20. 540

21. 112

22. 485

23. 600

24. 49

25. 914

26. 390

27. 825

Addition

1.
```
  T U
  2 4
+ 1 3
_____

_____
```

2.
```
  T U
  6 4
+ 1 4
_____

_____
```

3.
```
  T U
  1 1
+ 4 6
_____

_____
```

4.
```
  T U
  3 2
+ 6 5
_____

_____
```

5.
```
  T U
  7 5
+ 2 2
_____

_____
```

6.
```
  T U
  1 6
+ 5 1
_____

_____
```

7.
```
  T U
  1 3
+ 3 6
_____

_____
```

8.
```
  T U
  5 4
+ 2 5
_____

_____
```

9.
```
  T U
  1 7
+   9
_____

_____
```

10.
```
  T U
  3 5
+ 1 6
_____

_____
```

11.
```
  T U
  8 0
+ 1 9
_____

_____
```

12.
```
  T U
  4 6
+ 2 6
_____

_____
```

13.
```
  T U
  3 9
+ 4 7
_____

_____
```

14.
```
  T U
  1 3
+ 7 7
_____

_____
```

15.
```
  T U
  2 3
+ 1 9
_____

_____
```

16.
```
  T U
  5 8
+ 3 7
_____

_____
```

17.
```
  T U
  6 9
+ 3 2
_____

_____
```

18.
```
  T U
  4 5
+ 7 8
_____

_____
```

19.
```
  T U
  3 3
+ 7 9
_____

_____
```

20.
```
  T U
  3 6
+ 9 7
_____

_____
```

8

1. ```
   H T U
   1 4 7
   +  2 2
   ─────
   ```

2. ```
   H T U
   2 5 4
   +  3 3
   ─────
   ```

3. ```
   H T U
     4 1
   + 1 0 7
   ─────
   ```

4. ```
   H T U
     6 0
   + 2 2 4
   ─────
   ```

5. ```
   H T U
   3 5 2
   + 1 2 7
   ─────
   ```

6. ```
   H T U
   2 8 4
   + 1 1 9
   ─────
   ```

7. ```
   H T U
   2 0 9
   + 1 8 4
   ─────
   ```

8. ```
   H T U
   1 7 3
   +  9 9
   ─────
   ```

9. ```
   H T U
   1 6 4
   + 2 8 7
   ─────
   ```

10. ```
   H T U
   2 6 1
   + 1 8 3
   ─────
   ```

11. ```
   H T U
   4 4 8
   + 9 5
   ─────
   ```

12. ```
   H T U
   3 0 8
   + 1 9 5
   ─────
   ```

13. ```
   H T U
   4 2 6
   + 1 7 8
   ─────
   ```

14. ```
   H T U
   3 8 8
   +  7 6
   ─────
   ```

15. ```
   H T U
     6 2
   + 1 5 9
   ─────
   ```

16. ```
   H T U
   3 0 8
   + 2 9 6
   ─────
   ```

17. ```
   H T U
   2 0 0
   + 1 6 4
   ─────
   ```

18. ```
   H T U
   2 8 8
   + 1 6 9
   ─────
   ```

19. ```
   H T U
   2 6 6
   + 1 4 8
   ─────
   ```

20. ```
   H T U
   1 8 8
   +  7 7
   ─────
   ```

Addition

Tom had a game of hoopla with his friends.
How many did each person score?

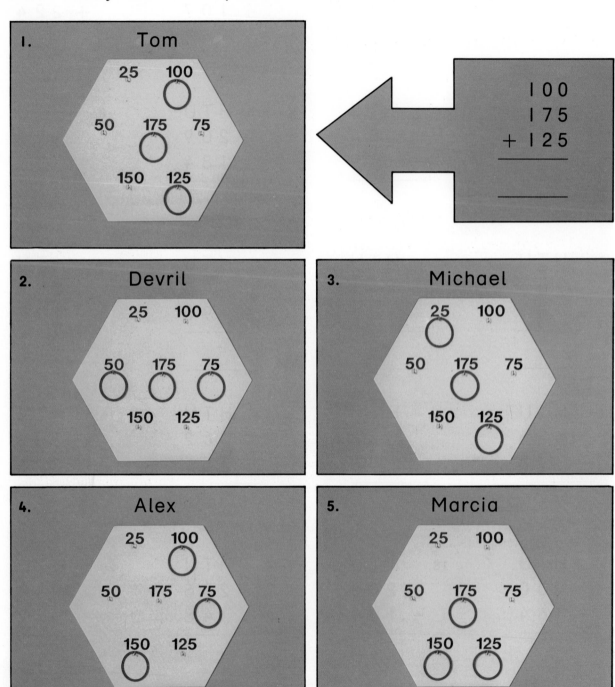

1. Tom

25   100
50   175   75
150   125

100
175
+ 125
_____

_____

2. Devril

25   100
50   175   75
150   125

3. Michael

25   100
50   175   75
150   125

4. Alex

25   100
50   175   75
150   125

5. Marcia

25   100
50   175   75
150   125

1. Find the total of 164 and 287.

2. Add together 73 and 185.

3. Find the sum of 96 and 248.

4. 293 plus 187.

5. 43 add 295.

6. Add 105 to 287.

In Pam's street there are:

73 houses
47 children
128 adults
36 pets

In Lynne's street there are:

85 houses
79 children
194 adults
44 pets

7. Find the total number of houses in both streets.

8. Find the total number of pets in both streets.

9. Find the total number of children in both streets.

10. Find the total number of adults in both streets.

11. Find the total number of people in both streets.

Length

Each space is called I **centimetre (cm)**.

Measure the length of each of these:

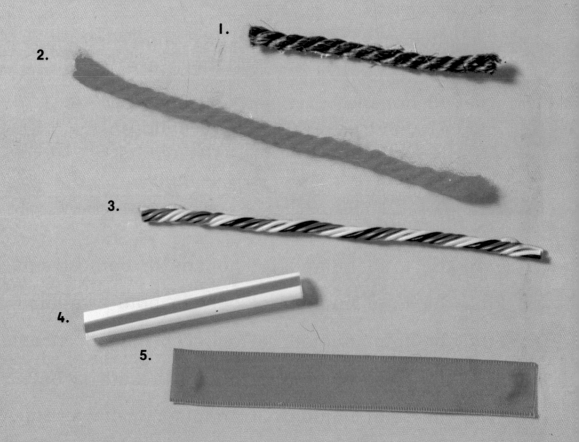

12

Measure the length of each of these:

1.

2.

3.

4.

Draw lines of length:

5. 8 cm   6. 10 cm   7. 3 cm   8. 5 cm

9. 7 cm   10. 6 cm   11. 11 cm   12. 13 cm

13

Tape measure

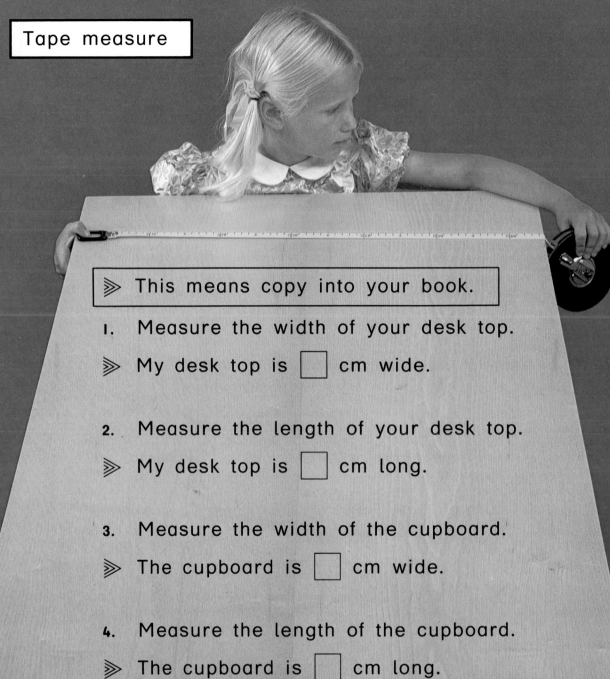

> ≫ This means copy into your book.

1. Measure the width of your desk top.

   ≫ My desk top is ☐ cm wide.

2. Measure the length of your desk top.

   ≫ My desk top is ☐ cm long.

3. Measure the width of the cupboard.

   ≫ The cupboard is ☐ cm wide.

4. Measure the length of the cupboard.

   ≫ The cupboard is ☐ cm long.

> Tape measure, ruler, P.E. cane, book

1. Guess the length of this toothbrush.

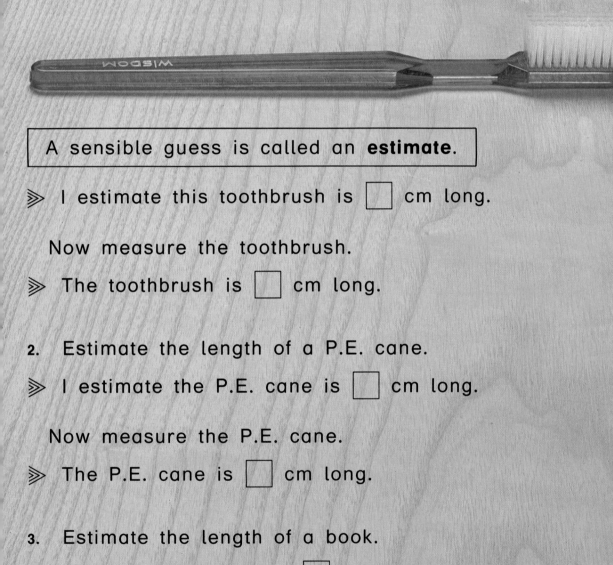

> A sensible guess is called an **estimate**.

≫ I estimate this toothbrush is ☐ cm long.

Now measure the toothbrush.

≫ The toothbrush is ☐ cm long.

2. Estimate the length of a P.E. cane.

≫ I estimate the P.E. cane is ☐ cm long.

Now measure the P.E. cane.

≫ The P.E. cane is ☐ cm long.

3. Estimate the length of a book.

≫ I estimate the book is ☐ cm long.

Now measure the book.

≫ The book is ☐ cm long.

Subtraction

Put 36 on your place value sheet.
Subtract 22.

Take away the 2 units first.
Then take away the 2 tens.

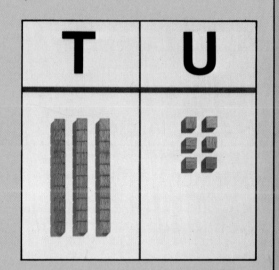

```
  T U
  3 6
- 2 2
------
  1 4
```

There are 14 left.

Remember to take away the units first.

1.
```
  T U
  3 8
- 2 1
------
```

2.
```
  T U
  5 7
- 2 5
------
```

3.
```
  T U
  4 7
- 2 6
------
```

4.
```
  T U
  3 5
- 1 2
------
```

5.
```
  T U
  7 6
- 5 1
------
```

6.
```
  T U
  4 6
- 2 6
------
```

7.
```
  T U
  2 7
- 1 0
------
```

8.
```
  T U
  4 2
- 3 1
------
```

9. T U
      3 3
    − 1 0
    ――――

10. T U
      6 4
    − 3 1
    ――――

11. T U
      4 3
    − 2 2
    ――――

12. T U
      5 2
    − 4 1
    ――――

13. T U
      2 8
    − 1 5
    ――――

14. T U
      5 6
    − 4 4
    ――――

15. T U
      5 8
    − 2 8
    ――――

16. T U
      6 3
    − 5 1
    ――――

17. T U
      7 7
    − 5 4
    ――――

18. T U
      4 9
    − 3 8
    ――――

19. T U
      8 9
    − 5 2
    ――――

20. T U
      6 8
    − 4 6
    ――――

21. T U
      8 8
    − 6 3
    ――――

22. T U
      6 9
    − 2 7
    ――――

23. T U
      5 4
    − 3 0
    ――――

24. T U
      8 5
    − 6 5
    ――――

25. T U
      8 6
    − 4 6
    ――――

26. T U
      9 5
    − 5 1
    ――――

27. T U
      9 8
    − 4 2
    ――――

28. T U
      6 6
    − 3 5
    ――――

Base 10 apparatus, place value sheet

Put 24 on your place value sheet.

T	U

Subtract 18.

```
T U
2 4
- 1 8
_____
```

There are not enough units.

Change a ten into units.

```
   1 14
 2 4
- 1 8
_____
```

T	U

Now take 8 units away.

There are 6 left.

Now take the 10 away.

```
   1 14
 2 4
- 1 8
_____
   6
```

T	U

1. 24
    − 19
    ───────

    ───────

2. 35
    − 26
    ───────

    ───────

3. 65
    − 48
    ───────

    ───────

4. 38
    − 29
    ───────

    ───────

5. 94
    − 36
    ───────

    ───────

6. 82
    − 58
    ───────

    ───────

7. 96
    − 59
    ───────

    ───────

8. 51
    − 25
    ───────

    ───────

9. 20
    − 16
    ───────

    ───────

10. 44
    − 27
    ───────

    ───────

11. 52
    − 38
    ───────

    ───────

12. 85
    − 67
    ───────

    ───────

13. 90
    − 41
    ───────

    ───────

14. 77
    − 28
    ───────

    ───────

15. 31
    − 15
    ───────

    ───────

16. 84
    − 49
    ───────

    ───────

17. 46
    − 27
    ───────

    ───────

18. 70
    − 43
    ───────

    ───────

19. 33
    − 14
    ───────

    ───────

20. 80
    − 51
    ───────

    ───────

21. 36
    − 17
    ───────

    ───────

22. 83
    − 46
    ───────

    ───────

23. 70
    − 24
    ───────

    ───────

24. 72
    − 28
    ───────

    ───────

Subtraction

Remember to take away the units first.

1. 50
    − 27
    _____

    _____

2. 42
    − 17
    _____

    _____

3. 33
    − 18
    _____

    _____

4. 40
    − 21
    _____

    _____

5. 63
    − 47
    _____

    _____

6. 53
    − 27
    _____

    _____

7. 76
    − 48
    _____

    _____

8. 37
    − 29
    _____

    _____

9. 93
    − 56
    _____

    _____

10. 75
    − 48
    _____

    _____

11. 43
    − 18
    _____

    _____

12. 61
    − 26
    _____

    _____

13. 57
    − 18
    _____

    _____

14. 63
    − 25
    _____

    _____

15. 47
    − 38
    _____

    _____

16. 74
    − 27
    _____

    _____

17. 60
    − 21
    _____

    _____

18. 56
    − 37
    _____

    _____

19. 73
    − 18
    _____

    _____

20. 83
    − 45
    _____

    _____

1. 46 − 18   2. 39 − 17   3. 51 − 26

4. 39 − 8   5. 50 − 37   6. 88 − 29

7. From 73 take 29.

8. Subtract 37 from 52.

9. 30 minus 16.

10. Which number is 17 less than 41?

11. How much greater than 24 is 72?

Mr. White is a milkman.
This list shows how many bottles he delivers.

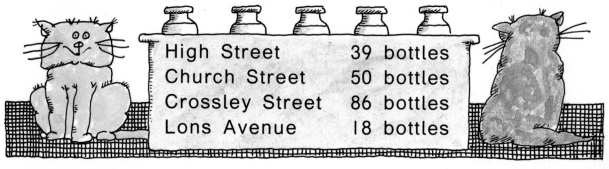

High Street	39 bottles
Church Street	50 bottles
Crossley Street	86 bottles
Lons Avenue	18 bottles

12. How many more bottles does he deliver in Church Street than in Lons Avenue?

13. How many more bottles does he deliver in Crossley Street than in High Street?

14. How many fewer bottles does he deliver in Lons Avenue than in Crossley Street?

15. How many fewer bottles does he deliver in High Street then in Church Street?

1. How much older than John is Sally?
2. How much older than Timothy is his father?
3. How much older than Sally is her grandfather?
4. How much older than Mr. Johnson is grandfather?

Great-Grandfather 91 years

Mr. Johnson (father)
35 years

Mrs. Johnson (mother)
33 years

Great-Grandmother
90 years

John
2 years

5. How much younger than great-grandfather is Timothy?

6. How much younger than Mrs. Johnson is Sally?

7. How much younger than great-grandmother is John?

8. How much younger than grandfather Johnson is Mrs. Johnson?

Sally
11 years

Grandfather
Johnson
60 years

Grandmother
Johnson
58 years

Timothy
7 years

Shape

These are tessellating patterns.
They leave no gaps.

Shapes that fit with no gaps **tessellate**.

Find shapes which make tessellating patterns.

Draw patterns with them.

24

1. There are ☐ rectangles.

2. There are ☐ squares.

3. There are ☐ circles.

4. There are ☐ triangles.

Solid shapes

These are **triangular prisms**.

These are **cones**.

Find some triangular prisms.

Will they roll?

Will they stack?

Find some cones.

Will they roll?

Will they stack?

1. How many cones can you see?
2. How many triangular prisms can you see?
3. How many cubes can you see?
4. How many cylinders can you see?
5. How many spheres can you see?
6. How many cuboids can you see?

Multiplication

Spot the missing numbers.

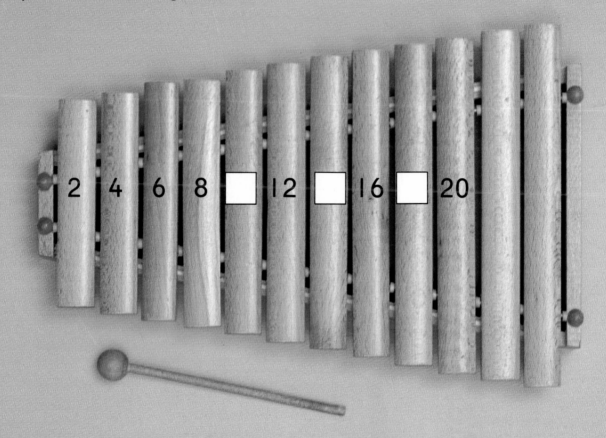

2 4 6 8 ☐ 12 ☐ 16 ☐ 20

Now do these:

1. 6, 8, 10, 12, ☐, ☐, ☐.

2. 4, ☐, 8, ☐, 12, ☐, 16.

3. ☐, ☐, 16, 18, 20.

Copy this on squared paper.

1	2	3	4	5	6	7	8	9	10
11	12	13	14	15	16	17	18	19	20
21	22	23	24	25	26	27	28	29	30
31	32	33	34	35	36	37	38	39	40
41	42	43	44	45	46	47	48	49	50

Stick it in your book.
Colour square 5.
Then colour square 10.
Keep on adding 5 and colour the square.

Make a 100 square.
Stick it in your book.
Colour square 10.
Add 10 each time and colour the square.

Now do these:

1. 5, 10, 15, ☐, ☐.

2. 10, 20, 30, ☐, ☐.

3. 25, 30, ☐, ☐, 45.

4. 20, 30, ☐, ☐, 60.

5. ☐, ☐, 25, 30.

6. ☐, 50, ☐, 70, 80.

Capacity

Litre jug, cup, jar, beaker, bottle, dish, funnel

Fill the litre jug with water.

Remember: a sensible guess is called an **estimate**.
≫ This means copy into your book.

1. Estimate how many cups 1 litre fills.

   ≫ I estimate 1 litre fills ☐ cups.

   Find out how many cups 1 litre fills.

   ≫ 1 litre fills ☐ cups.

2. ≫ I estimate I· litre fills ☐ jars.

Find out how many jars I litre fills.

≫ I litre fills ☐ jars.

3. ≫ I estimate I litre fills ☐ beakers.

Find out how many beakers I litre fills.

≫ I litre fills ☐ beakers.

4. ≫ I estimate I litre fills ☐ bottles.

Find out how many bottles I litre fills.

≫ I litre fills ☐ bottles.

5. ≫ I estimate I litre fills ☐ dishes.

Find out how many dishes I litre fills.

≫ I litre fills ☐ dishes.

Fractions

Fold the square like this:

Open it.
It looks like this:

Each part is called a **half**.

Half is written like this: $\frac{1}{2}$

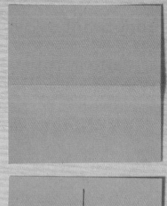

Write $\frac{1}{2}$ in each part.

Fold the circle in half.

Write $\frac{1}{2}$ in each part.

Stick the shapes in your book.

≫ $\frac{1}{2} + \frac{1}{2} = 1$ whole one.

32

Plane shapes, gummed paper, scissors

Find a triangle.
Put it on the gummed paper.
Draw round it.
Cut it out.

Fold the triangle in half.
Cut along the fold.

Write $\frac{1}{2}$ in each part.

Stick each half in your book.

≫ $\frac{1}{2} + \frac{1}{2} = 1$ whole one.

Do the same with a rectangle.

Plane shapes

Draw two squares.

Draw a line on each square to halve it
in a different way, like this:

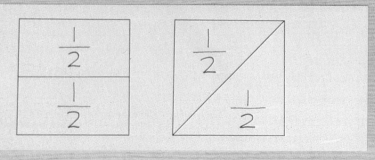

Write $\frac{1}{2}$ in each part.

Find a rectangle.
Draw it twice.
Draw a line on each rectangle to halve it
in a different way.

Write $\frac{1}{2}$ in each part.

≫ $\frac{1}{2} + \frac{1}{2} = 1$ whole.

Gummed paper square and circle

Fold the square like this: Fold it again like this:

Open it.
It looks like this:

Each part is called a **quarter**.

Quarter is written like this: $\frac{1}{4}$

Write $\frac{1}{4}$ in each part.

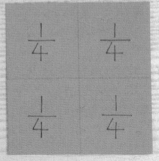

Fold the circle into quarters.

Write $\frac{1}{4}$ in each part.

Stick both shapes in your book.

$\gg \frac{1}{4} + \frac{1}{4} + \frac{1}{4} + \frac{1}{4} = 1$ whole one.

Weight

Balance, set of weights, peas, marbles, beads,
counters and bottle tops

Find these weights.

These are for weighing with.

We weigh in **grams**.

20 g means 20 grams.

50 g means 50 grams.

100 g means 100 grams.

1. Which is the lightest weight?

2. Which is the heaviest weight?

Put the 20 g weight in one pan.
Fill the other pan with peas until they balance.
Write in your book how many peas balance 20 g.
Now do the same again with counters.

Change the 20 g weight for the 50 g.
Write how many marbles weigh 50 g.
Write how many beads weigh 50 g.
Write how many metal bottle tops weigh 50 g.

Change the 50 g weight for the 100 g.
Guess how many marbles weigh 100 g.

Remember: a sensible guess is called an **estimate**.

Write how many marbles weigh 100 g.
Do the same again with beads.

Division

Base 10 apparatus

Divide 24 into 2 equal groups.

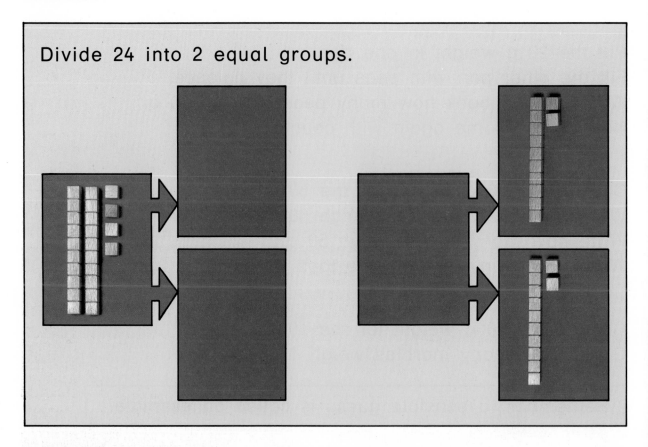

Do these in the same way.

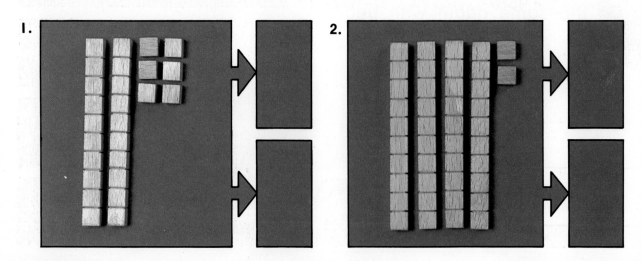

1.

2.

38

Division

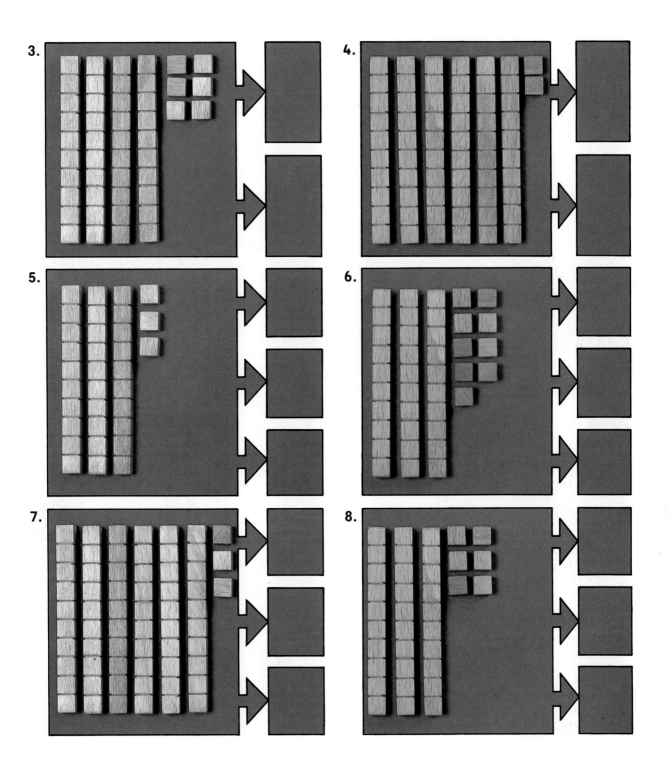

39

Money

Coins

John's mother went shopping.
She bought an apple, a pear
and 2 oranges.

This is what it cost her.

She paid 21p altogether.

Use your coins to find the cost of:

1. a bunch of bananas, an apple and a pear.
2. 2 lemons, a bunch of grapes and an apple.
3. a pear, an orange and two apples.
4. an orange, a pear, an apple and a bunch of bananas.
5. a bunch of grapes and a bunch of bananas.
6. 2 oranges, 2 pears and 3 apples.

Here is a picture of a 50p piece.

These coins are worth 50p altogether.

Draw another set of coins which is worth 50p altogether.
Find 2 more ways of making 50p.

Coins

Mary has 50p pocket money each week.

How much will she have left if she buys:

1. ?

2. ?

3. ?

4. ?

5. ?

6. ?

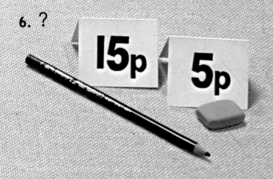

Time

Clock stamp

Write the times these clocks show.

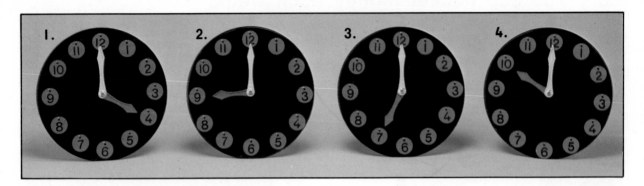

Stamp 4 clock faces.
Make the clocks show these times.

5. 2 o'clock

6. 11 o'clock

7. 6 o'clock

8. 8 o'clock

I hour later

I hour is 60 minutes.

≫ I hour = 60 minutes.

These clocks show:

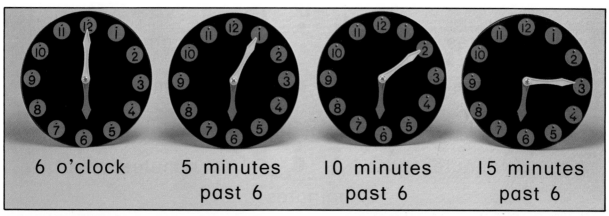

6 o'clock — 5 minutes past 6 — 10 minutes past 6 — 15 minutes past 6

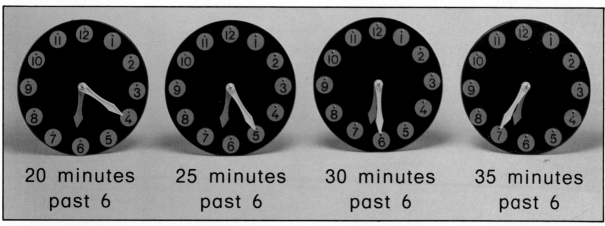

20 minutes past 6 — 25 minutes past 6 — 30 minutes past 6 — 35 minutes past 6

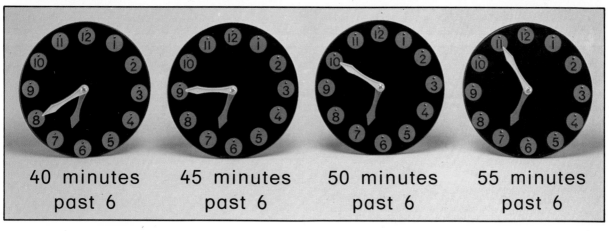

40 minutes past 6 — 45 minutes past 6 — 50 minutes past 6 — 55 minutes past 6

Clock stamp

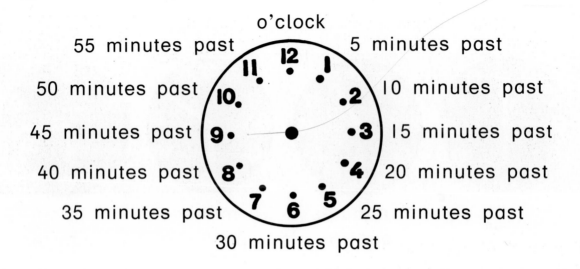

Write the times these clocks show.

1. ☐ minutes past 10
2. ☐ minutes past 11
3. ☐ minutes past 9
4. ☐ minutes past 7

5. ☐ minutes past ☐
6. ☐ minutes past ☐
7. ☐ minutes past ☐
8. ☐ minutes past ☐

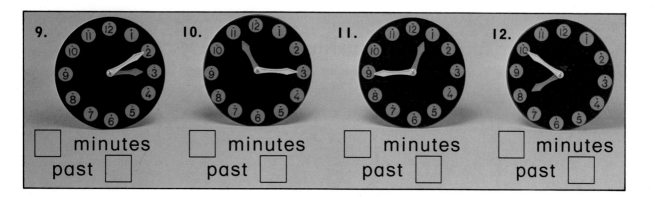

9. ☐ minutes past ☐

10. ☐ minutes past ☐

11. ☐ minutes past ☐

12. ☐ minutes past ☐

Stamp 8 clock faces.
Make the clocks show these times.

13. 5 minutes past 4.   14. 55 minutes past 8.

15. 45 minutes past 6.   16. 15 minutes past 1.

17. 30 minutes past 9.   18. 40 minutes past 2.

19. 10 minutes past 3.   20. 50 minutes past 4.

Write these times in your book.

21. The time you get out of bed.

22. The time school starts in the morning.

23. The time you have dinner.

24. The time you leave school.

25. The time you go to bed.

47

Graphs

John asked his class which lollipops they liked best.
The graph shows what he found out.

Graph to show favourite lollipops

Number of children (vertical axis: 0, 1, 2, 3, 4, 5, 6)

Flavour (horizontal axis): raspberry, strawberry, chocolate, lime, banana, orange

Find these answers from the graph.

1. Which flavour did the children like most?

2. Which flavour did the children like least?

3. How many children liked raspberry flavour best?

4. How many children liked strawberry flavour best?

5. How many children liked banana flavour best?

6. The same number of children chose two flavours. Which flavours were they?

7. How many children did John ask altogether?

Squared paper

John asked his class which games they liked best.
This table shows what he found out.

Game	Number of children
Football	6
Hide and seek	4
Rounders	5
Cricket	2
Marbles	4
Hop scotch	3

Copy this on a piece of squared paper.
Remember to put in the labels.

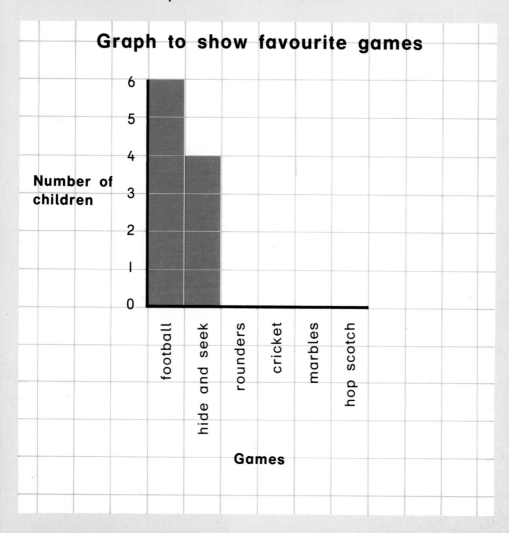

Graph to show favourite games

Number of children

Games

Finish the graph from the table on the opposite page.
The graph you have drawn is called a **column graph**.

Investigations

Elastic bands, 9-pin geo-board, spotty paper

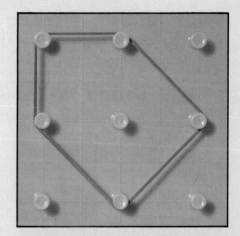

Make different shapes.
Each shape must have I nail
inside it.
How many shapes can you find?
Draw each shape on spotty paper.

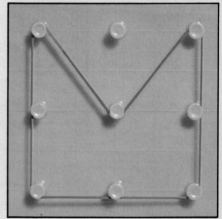

Make shapes with 5 sides.
Each shape must have no nails
inside it.
How many shapes can you find?
Draw each shape on spotty paper.

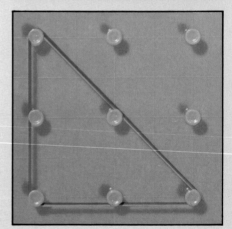

Make different triangles.
How many can you find?
Draw each triangle on spotty paper.

Cuisenaire rods or Stern rods

Put the 4 rod on your desk.

Match it with two rods like this:

2 + 2

3 + 1

1 + 3

There are three ways of matching it using two rods.

How many ways are there of matching it using three rods?
How many ways are there of matching it using four rods?

Put the 5 rod on your desk.

How many ways are there of matching it using:

two rods?
three rods?
four rods?
five rods?

Problem Page

1. Robert collects toy cars.
   He has 24 red ones, 19 green ones and 7 blue ones.
   How many has he altogether?

2. Jane enjoys baking with her mother.
   One day they baked 18 jam tarts, 12 lemon curd tarts and 18 treacle tarts.
   How many tarts did they bake altogether?

3. In Jane's village there are 84 children.
   48 of them are boys.
   How many girls are there?

4. The village cinema holds 92 people.
   Last night there were 24 empty seats.
   How many people went to the cinema last night?

5. A library van visits the village each week.
   Last week 58 children and 109 adults changed books at the van.
   How many people visited the library van last week?

6. Mr. Smart, the baker, sells 85 loaves a day.
   47 loaves are not sliced.
   How many sliced loaves does he sell each day?

7. At the village cricket match there were 125 men,
   48 women and 39 children.
   How many people went to the cricket match?

8. Colin and Philip deliver papers in the village.
   Colin delivers 70 papers each day.
   Philip delivers 45 papers each day.
   How many more papers does Colin deliver than
   Philip each day?

9. Mr. Richards, the farmer, has 73 cows.
   45 of them are in the cow shed.
   How many are left in the field?

10. As well as the 73 cows, Mr. Richards has 78 sheep,
    26 pigs and 3 dogs.
    How many animals has he altogether?

Addition – more practice

1. 54
    + 26
    ――――

    ――――

2. 73
    + 19
    ――――

    ――――

3. 14
    + 88
    ――――

    ――――

4. 29
    + 35
    ――――

    ――――

5. 94
    + 78
    ――――

    ――――

6. 69
    + 36
    ――――

    ――――

7. 49
    + 128
    ――――

    ――――

8. 307
    + 145
    ――――

    ――――

9. 428
    + 107
    ――――

    ――――

10. 217
    + 135
    ――――

    ――――

11. 872
    + 119
    ――――

    ――――

12. 534
    + 137
    ――――

    ――――

13. 242
    + 193
    ――――

    ――――

14. 580
    + 195
    ――――

    ――――

15. 93
    + 141
    ――――

    ――――

16. 724
    + 85
    ――――

    ――――

17. 247
    + 590
    ――――

    ――――

18. 791
    + 197
    ――――

    ――――

19. 69
    + 190
    ――――

    ――――

20. 487
    + 392
    ――――

    ――――

21. 693
    + 217
    ――――

    ――――

22. 402
    + 319
    ――――

    ――――

23. 568
    + 92
    ――――

    ――――

24. 720
    + 181
    ――――

    ――――

1. 346
    + 174
    _____

2. 407
    + 197
    _____

3. 319
    + 284
    _____

4. 633
    + 94
    _____

5. 642
    + 198
    _____

6. 243
    + 694
    _____

7. 389
    + 574
    _____

8. 572
    + 368
    _____

9. 241
    + 699
    _____

10. 704
    + 198
    _____

11. 582
    + 375
    _____

12. 228
    + 174
    _____

13. 427
    + 178
    _____

14. 589
    + 109
    _____

15. 312
    + 147
    _____

16. 94
    + 89
    _____

17. 638
    + 195
    _____

18. 657
    + 268
    _____

19. 426
    + 394
    _____

20. 598
    + 189
    _____

21. 705
    + 196
    _____

22. 428
    + 419
    _____

23. 668
    + 247
    _____

24. 395
    + 86
    _____

Addition — more practice

1.   495
  + 225
_____

2.   617
  + 198
_____

3.   307
  + 298
_____

4.   248
  + 164
_____

5.   87
  + 499
_____

6.   523
  + 247
_____

7.   391
  + 472
_____

8.   305
  + 289
_____

9.   779
  + 48
_____

10.   644
  + 187
_____

11.   397
  + 294
_____

12.   530
  + 192
_____

13.   592
  + 49
_____

14.   29
  + 191
_____

15.   318
  + 329
_____

16.   483
  + 184
_____

17.   291
  + 419
_____

18.   304
  + 97
_____

19.   128
  + 484
_____

20.   342
  + 179
_____

21.   750
  + 154
_____

22.   697
  + 217
_____

23.   227
  + 595
_____

24.   381
  + 139
_____

Subtraction – more practice

1. 53
 − 26
 ⎯⎯

2. 80
 − 41
 ⎯⎯

3. 89
 − 53
 ⎯⎯

4. 93
 − 46
 ⎯⎯

5. 46
 − 16
 ⎯⎯

6. 74
 − 35
 ⎯⎯

7. 98
 − 69
 ⎯⎯

8. 75
 − 48
 ⎯⎯

9. 71
 − 62
 ⎯⎯

10. 40
 − 25
 ⎯⎯

11. 92
 − 46
 ⎯⎯

12. 78
 − 54
 ⎯⎯

13. 95
 − 58
 ⎯⎯

14. 51
 − 37
 ⎯⎯

15. 73
 − 64
 ⎯⎯

16. 84
 − 15
 ⎯⎯

17. 86
 − 55
 ⎯⎯

18. 34
 − 7
 ⎯⎯

19. 57
 − 48
 ⎯⎯

20. 63
 − 28
 ⎯⎯

21. 95
 − 35
 ⎯⎯

22. 47
 − 18
 ⎯⎯

23. 70
 − 39
 ⎯⎯

24. 87
 − 59
 ⎯⎯

Subtraction – more practice

1.
$$\begin{array}{r} 50 \\ -17 \\ \hline \\ \hline \end{array}$$

2.
$$\begin{array}{r} 63 \\ -24 \\ \hline \\ \hline \end{array}$$

3.
$$\begin{array}{r} 28 \\ -14 \\ \hline \\ \hline \end{array}$$

4.
$$\begin{array}{r} 73 \\ -55 \\ \hline \\ \hline \end{array}$$

5.
$$\begin{array}{r} 74 \\ -24 \\ \hline \\ \hline \end{array}$$

6.
$$\begin{array}{r} 40 \\ -12 \\ \hline \\ \hline \end{array}$$

7.
$$\begin{array}{r} 57 \\ -48 \\ \hline \\ \hline \end{array}$$

8.
$$\begin{array}{r} 91 \\ -25 \\ \hline \\ \hline \end{array}$$

9.
$$\begin{array}{r} 55 \\ -36 \\ \hline \\ \hline \end{array}$$

10.
$$\begin{array}{r} 90 \\ -45 \\ \hline \\ \hline \end{array}$$

11.
$$\begin{array}{r} 62 \\ -25 \\ \hline \\ \hline \end{array}$$

12.
$$\begin{array}{r} 34 \\ -17 \\ \hline \\ \hline \end{array}$$

13.
$$\begin{array}{r} 82 \\ -64 \\ \hline \\ \hline \end{array}$$

14.
$$\begin{array}{r} 79 \\ -54 \\ \hline \\ \hline \end{array}$$

15.
$$\begin{array}{r} 50 \\ -14 \\ \hline \\ \hline \end{array}$$

16.
$$\begin{array}{r} 78 \\ -69 \\ \hline \\ \hline \end{array}$$

17.
$$\begin{array}{r} 65 \\ -48 \\ \hline \\ \hline \end{array}$$

18.
$$\begin{array}{r} 48 \\ -9 \\ \hline \\ \hline \end{array}$$

19.
$$\begin{array}{r} 43 \\ -19 \\ \hline \\ \hline \end{array}$$

20.
$$\begin{array}{r} 93 \\ -45 \\ \hline \\ \hline \end{array}$$

21.
$$\begin{array}{r} 30 \\ -26 \\ \hline \\ \hline \end{array}$$

22.
$$\begin{array}{r} 74 \\ -48 \\ \hline \\ \hline \end{array}$$

23.
$$\begin{array}{r} 81 \\ -33 \\ \hline \\ \hline \end{array}$$

24.
$$\begin{array}{r} 52 \\ -14 \\ \hline \\ \hline \end{array}$$

1. 66
  − 27
  _____

  _____

2. 31
  − 8
  _____

  _____

3. 45
  − 16
  _____

  _____

4. 72
  − 36
  _____

  _____

5. 77
  − 51
  _____

  _____

6. 97
  − 88
  _____

  _____

7. 88
  − 69
  _____

  _____

8. 50
  − 47
  _____

  _____

9. 38
  − 24
  _____

  _____

10. 56
  − 38
  _____

  _____

11. 71
  − 54
  _____

  _____

12. 94
  − 69
  _____

  _____

13. 83
  − 67
  _____

  _____

14. 90
  − 41
  _____

  _____

15. 45
  − 27
  _____

  _____

16. 50
  − 36
  _____

  _____

17. 94
  − 35
  _____

  _____

18. 84
  − 36
  _____

  _____

19. 52
  − 32
  _____

  _____

20. 66
  − 48
  _____

  _____

21. 62
  − 39
  _____

  _____

22. 77
  − 58
  _____

  _____

23. 42
  − 15
  _____

  _____

24. 88
  − 39
  _____

  _____

Assessment

1. Write five hundred and one in figures.

2. Write the value of the number in red. 43 6

3. 473
   + 294
   _____

   _____

4. 801
   + 99
   _____

   _____

5.   49
   + 262
   _____

   _____

6. Mr. Adam took 38 boys and 15 girls to the museum. How many children did he take?

Measure these lines.

7. _____

8. _____

9. Draw a line 5 cm long.

10. Draw a line 9 cm long.

11. 47
   − 29
   _____

   _____

12. 62
   − 35
   _____

   _____

13.   50
   − 18
   _____

   _____

14. Simon has 34 records.
   Lisa has 17 records.
   How many more records has Simon than Lisa?

Name these shapes.

15.

16.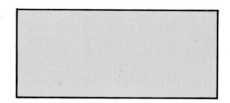

17.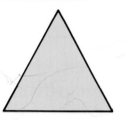

18.

19.

20.

21. $\dfrac{1}{2} + \boxed{} = 1$ whole one.

22. $\dfrac{1}{4} + \dfrac{1}{4} + \dfrac{1}{4} + \dfrac{1}{4} = \boxed{}$

23.

$\boxed{}$ minutes past $\boxed{}$

24.

$\boxed{}$ minutes past $\boxed{}$

Glossary

abacus

abaci   more than one abacus

centimetre   a measure of length

cone

circle

cube

cuboid

cylinder

estimate   a sensible guess

gram   a measure of weight

litre   a measure of liquid

rectangle

sphere

square

tessellate   to fit shapes together without gaps

triangle

triangular prism